I0436203

Latham and The Link
A Legacy of Cruelty Prevention
and
Personal Responsibility

By

Phil Arkow

Copyright © 2012

The Latham Foundation for the Promotion of Humane Education

All rights reserved.

ISBN - 13: 978 – 1479369843
ISBN – 10: 1479369845

DEDICATION

This book is dedicated to all the women, children, and animals who suffer violence at the hands of abusers, and to the pioneering leaders in animal care and control, domestic violence, children protection, and elder abuse who work tirelessly to give voice to the voiceless. These innovators recognize the fact that violence against any family member puts all in the home and community at risk.

CONTENTS

ACKNOWLEDGMENTS

The Latham Foundation acknowledges the interest and support of the many local, state, national and international organizations, and individuals who have worked to conceptualize, promote, and implement The Link in programs and coalitions. In particular, we commend the American Humane Association, the American Society for the Prevention of Cruelty to Animals, the National Link Coalition, and many others too numerous to list for their pioneering efforts and commitment to the prevention of all forms of family and community violence.

1. THE START OF A LEGACY

When Oakland, Calif., humanitarians Edith Latham and her brother Milton Latham established The Latham Foundation for the Promotion of Humane Education in May, 1918, their goal was to encourage young people to adopt kind treatment of all living creatures. Humane education, then as now, inspires a sense of empathy and responsibility in children as a means of building moral character and promoting social and personal responsibility. Financially comfortable and independent with numerous interests, the Lathams had long been pet lovers. They were appalled at how horses were beaten in the streets and how animals were cruelly treated in the fledgling Hollywood film industry. These two highly educated and kindness-oriented individuals determined to devote their inheritance and the remainder of their lives to helping those who could not speak for themselves.

Like many people we admire, the Lathams were ahead of their time. With impressive foresight and generosity, they launched their Foundation "to foster a deeper understanding of and sympathy with man's relations – the animals." Yet their purpose was not merely to protect animals: their vision was tempered by a long historical tradition in which kindness to animals is as much about human well-being as about animal welfare, and merely the first of many steps to achieving healthy interpersonal relationships. The Foundation's purpose is:

- To inculcate the higher principles of humaneness upon which the unity and happiness of the world depend,

- To emphasize the spiritual fundamentals that lead to world friendship,

- To promote the character building of the child by an understanding of universal kinship, and

- To foster a deeper understanding of and sympathy with man's relations – the animals – who cannot speak for themselves.

Inherent in such language is the recognition that actions against the animals who share our homes, communities and planet affect human society as well, and that all forms of life – and all acts of violence against them – are interrelated.

More than 50 years ago, more than 40,000 children who joined the Brother Buzz Club took the following pledge:

"I will try to be kind to every living creature and to cultivate a spirit of protection toward all who are weaker than myself, and I will try to treat animals as I would wish to be treated if I were in their place."

The seeds that Edith and Milton Latham planted in 1918 have blossomed into a tree of life-affirming values. While the root of this tree remains humane education, today the tree has three additional branches: the therapeutic use of animals to help people in need; an appreciation for the attachments and many dimensions of the human-animal bond; and a greater understanding of the intersections between animal abuse and other forms of violence.

2. HUMANE EDUCATION AND THE LINK

Little Goody Two Shoes.

The Lathams brought forward a concept that had become widely popular 50 years earlier and that was poised for even greater receptivity by the public. Philosophers as far back as Ovid in ancient Rome and St. Thomas Aquinas in the 13th Century had promoted the idea that a child's kind or cruel treatment of animals was a strong indicator of how that child's character would develop as an adult. John Locke, in 1693, and William Hogarth, in 1751, gave impetus to the idea that promoting children's acts of kindness to animals would positively improve their character development. One of the first full-length children's books in the English language – *The History of Little Goody Two-Shoes,* written by an anonymous author in 1765 – further popularized this concept through heroine Margery Meanwell who helped mistreated animals.

Children's literature in the Victorian Era frequently offered moral lessons in which good children cared for animals, and bad children were those who were unkind. It did not take long for this idea to manifest itself in the newly-formed humane movement, which arrived in America in 1866. By 1868, George T. Angell founded the Massachusetts SPCA and quickly identified "humane education" as the intervention of choice for guiding wayward youths into a righteous path in which animals were well regarded, respected and cared for – not just for the animals' welfare, but to improve human behavior. Three founders of the early humane movement – Angell in Boston, Henry Bergh in New York, and Caroline Earle White in Philadelphia – outspokenly believed that the focal job of a humane society should be moral education and public advocacy rather than rescuing and sheltering animals.

Humane education was seen as a means of insulating youth, and boys in particular, against cruel tendencies that might undermine civic life. Caring for animals became an important model for inculcating standards of gentility such as self-discipline, Christian sentiment, empathy, and moral sensitivity. As the Lathams were defining their values, humane education was seen as even broader in scope, with kindness toward animals eventually leading to universal peace and a brotherhood of man.

The Latham Foundation's founding and ongoing principles exemplify this paradigm. A poster from the 1930s, created by Miriam de Lemos, depicts two children with a puppy approaching a set of steps leading to "world friendship." The first step up this hill is "kindness to animals," which will subsequently take the voyagers to kindness to each other, other people, our country, other nations, and the world.

Domestic violence, child abuse, and elder abuse do not specifically appear on the Latham "steps." Yet families are part of a child's environment, and it is becoming increasingly obvious that violence against any family member – whether with two legs or four – is a step away from our values of universal kinship and respect for all life. Cruelty to animals perpetrated by any family member is often an indicator and predictor of violence against other members of the family as well.

Latham has been promoting humane education for several generations. As new audiences have discovered humane education, Latham has adapted its message to meet the needs and interests of changing times and technology.

3. OUTREACH AND PARTNERSHIPS TO ADVANCE AWARENESS AND ACTION

As the first national organization devoted exclusively to humane education, Latham has long been a thought leader, innovator, and partner with organizations and individuals who share their commitment to promoting the well-being of people, animals, and the environment. While not a grant-making foundation, Latham serves as a producer of cutting-edge educational productions, a clearinghouse for information about humane issues and activities, and a catalyst for responsible thought and action.

From the outset, Latham has readapted and improved its approach by identifying the critical issues of the time and raising the profile of these issues through new technologies and culturally relevant messaging.

In the 1920s "traveling teachers" Gwyn Tebault and Dolores Wilkens Kent visited local schools promoting character-building and citizenship; their low-tech instructional flannel boards were the multimedia of the era. A monthly publication, *The Kind Deeds Messenger,* soon expanded the outreach. The Latham Kind Deeds Club, formed in 1925, quickly had over 10,000 members who promised to do two good deeds every day, one for an animal and one for another person.

Latham's outreach expanded dramatically in 1925 via international poster contests that continued into the 1960s. During the 1930s and 1940s as many as 40 poster exhibits, which attracted thousands of entries, were traveling around the country. By 1927 the Foundation was using the new medium of radio to produce regular broadcasts for children. Latham also provided scripts for schools to read over their classroom radio systems to teach children about respect for others.

The iconic puppet Brother Buzz, who had been the Foundation's spokesperson since 1927 in stories and on Saturday morning radio programs, made the transition to the then-new medium of television in 1952. *The Wonderful World of Brother Buzz* was the first children's program with humane education as its goal; it played a pivotal role in the development of children's TV programming. By 1953 more than 40,000 children had joined the Brother Buzz Club, pledging to be kind to every living creature and to cultivate a spirit of protection. The local Brother Buzz TV program, filmed using then state-of-the-art kinescope technology, was syndicated in 1957. Soon it was distributed nationally as a weekly children's series that aired until 1995. Brother Buzz and Miss Busy Bee, along with Mr. Blue Jay and Odie the Skunk, are in retirement today but they remain in the fond memory of all who grew up with them during their era.

Latham's "With-It" TV series evolved into a collection of science and adventure videos with study guides used by schools across the country. Latham began producing educational films in 16 mm format in 1958, and later converted them into videotape and digital formats, reaching millions of viewers worldwide and winning many awards for excellence.

The Latham Letter was first published in the Fall of 1980 to fill a unique niche: a publication of interest to academic researchers, non-academic professionals and the general public interested in animal issues and humane education.

As early as 1979 Latham Vice President Wallie Jamie, an executive with the Carnation Company, was among the first to describe a human/animal "bond." By 1980 Latham was helping to nurture the new interest in the therapeutic use of animals by taking the fledgling Delta Foundation of Portland, Ore., under its aegis. The Delta Group of The Latham Foundation promoted research and education on the human-animal bond. It sponsored a Symposium and Workshop at the University of Hawaii and a pioneering International Conference at the University of Pennsylvania in 1981. Later that year the Group became an

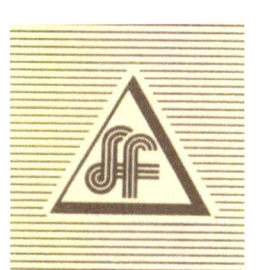

independent entity, known first as The Delta Society and today as Pet Partners, a world-renowned organization advancing human health and well-being through positive interactions with animals. Meanwhile, Latham's humane education materials swiftly grew to include video and publications. Additionally, Latham sponsored three national conferences on the "bond" and animal-assisted therapy.

As the 21st Century dawned, Latham became the virtual office of the new Association of Professional Humane Educators (formerly the Western Humane and Environmental Educators Association). Latham participated in the digital information revolution, with a Web presence vastly expanding awareness of the Foundation, particularly among foreign audiences. The Foundation digitized *Latham Letters,* making them instantly and freely available online. By

2009 one could find clips of many of Latham's educational videos on YouTube.

Inherent throughout all these innovations was a common thread: that man's interactions with animals have the potential to be mutually beneficial or mutually deleterious. In the groundbreaking 1984 book on animal-assisted therapy, *Dynamic Relationships in Practice: Animals in the Helping Professions,* Latham noted the underlying philosophy that had dictated its focus for decades and which continues, more than a quarter-century later, to drive its work:

"The Latham Foundation unequivocally believes that mankind is best served by a clear understanding of the vital importance of universal kinship and respect for all life. Latham believes that a child taught to respect animals and all living things will grow to respect his fellow man as well."

It was only natural to adapt this philosophy to a renaissance of interest in how animal cruelty, abuse and neglect are linked to other forms of family violence. By the late 1980s Latham had established itself as a pioneer in this arena as well.

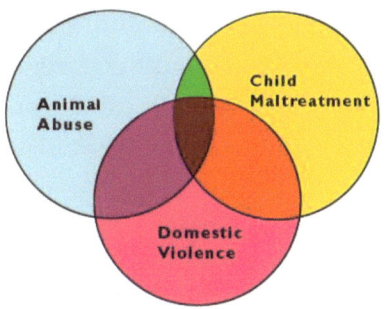

4. ADDRESSING THE CONNECTION

From inception, Latham has recognized that kindness to animals is a critical first step toward reducing aggression among people. While the prevention of family violence was not specifically identified in 1918, by the late 1980s Latham began to look at animal abuse in a new way. Latham began to assert that acts of animal cruelty are often the predictors and indicators of escalating acts of violence against the human members of the family. This model of preventing cruelty to animals was an updated paradigm that was more consonant with contemporary criminal justice and social services systems.

This new paradigm became what colleagues at the American Humane Association subsequently called "The Link" — the intersections of animal cruelty, domestic violence, child maltreatment, and elder abuse. For Latham, it was a natural extension of long-held beliefs: for example, a 1929 issue of *The Kind Deeds Messenger,* Latham's story service for public schools published from 1924 to 1945, noted how teaching kindness to animals could stave off antisocial behaviors. Jennie R. Nichols, National Humane Education Chair of the Parents and Teachers Association, wrote:

"Kindness is the one tongue that all human kind can understand and that all creatures may be made to feel. It is the language that holds the balance of power in settling difficulties between individuals and nations for, above all, a heart made kind means a mind above crime."

By the late 1980s Latham was exploring the next frontier of human-animal interactions: what was being called the "dark side" of the human-animal bond. There was growing evidence that in situations where child abuse exists, animal abuse is frequently also present, and vice versa. Social scientists were beginning to recognize that different forms of violence and abuse often stem from the same motivations and conditions, regardless of whether the victims are human or animal. Acts of cruelty, abuse and neglect to animals were again being seen as not only unacceptable behavior and injurious to animals, but also as adversely affecting human welfare. Yet paradoxically, few child welfare and animal protection agencies were exchanging information to help their case workers detect, reduce, and prevent maltreatment.

This was ironic, for the child protection movement had originated in animal welfare and humane societies had had dual missions in preventing both animal and child abuse for many decades. Yet over the years the fields had specialized and bifurcated to the point where contemporary organizations rarely communicated with each other, let alone provide cross-training and inter-agency referrals. Latham began to produce materials that encouraged human and humane services agencies to work together cooperatively to remedy a common problem.

The child and animal protection movements "forgot their historical roots," wrote Phil Arkow, Chair of Latham's newly-formed Child and Animal Abuse Prevention Project (CAAP) in the Fall, 1994 issue of *The Latham Letter*. "The compartmentalization approach hasn't worked. Maybe it's time to re-explore that old connection and see if we can get some synergy going by working together. Beginning about two years ago, we began looking at another component, which is that there are so many cases in which people are cruel to animals in one form or another, and that violence escalates against other vulnerable victims, whether they are children or spouses or other members of society."

Latham was quick to note that animal welfare is not more important than human welfare. "What we're saying is that violence is violence. The only thing that differs is whether the victim has two legs or four," Arkow said.

The Link describes these interpersonal and interspecies connections, summed up in this diagram first used in Latham's groundbreaking 1999 textbook, *Child Abuse, Domestic Violence, and Animal Abuse: Linking the Circles of Compassion for Prevention and Education,* edited by Phil Arkow and Frank Ascione. In this model, aspects of child maltreatment, animal cruelty and domestic violence have clear overlaps, and professionals in each field are encouraged to be on the lookout for the other forms of family violence that they may encounter. By cross-training officials and creating good working relationships, case workers may cross-report

Child Abuse, Domestic Violence, and Animal Abuse

Linking the Circles of Compassion for Prevention and Intervention

edited by Frank R. Ascione and Phil Arkow

their findings to corresponding agencies. Holistic coalitions that address all forms of violence work cooperatively to solve problems too large for any one field to address alone.

In recent years, this model has been expanded to include elder abuse as another form of family violence in which animals may be harmed. Similarly, adult protective services caseworkers are being trained to recognize and report parallel forms of abuse and neglect.

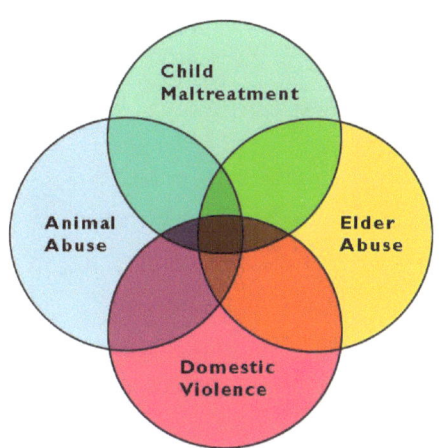

The conventional wisdom that childhood acts of animal cruelty predict adult acts of violence and criminality is now widely regarded by researchers as simplistic: animal cruelty is, rather, part of a complex constellation of antisocial behaviors that occur in no particular order and that may have similar underlying causes. Among the many findings that researchers have discovered are:

- Acts of animal cruelty perpetrated by children may precede violence in later life, particularly if those acts are persistent, severe and lacking in remorse or restraint.

- Animal abuse is highly prevalent in homes marked with child abuse, particularly physical child abuse.

- Childhood animal cruelty increases in homes where children have been abused or exposed to domestic violence.

- Significant numbers of domestic violence survivors report that their partners also threatened, harmed or killed animals to coerce, control or intimidate their victims and keep them trapped in violent relationships.

- Men who abuse both their partner and the family pet use more violence and controlling behaviors than do those who abuse only their partner.

- Offenders who are prosecuted for animal cruelty are more likely to have criminal records for other violent offenses.

- Family members may threaten to harm animals in order to coerce or control vulnerable seniors.

- Elders with limited resources may be unable to care for their pets adequately, or may neglect themselves in order to provide for their animals.

- A significant percentage of animal hoarders are seniors.

The complexities of these dynamics, and the interdisciplinary nature of family violence, combined with limitations on how research can be conducted and findings adapted into practical applications, make The Link an ongoing and fascinating challenge. Latham's purpose is to acquire and communicate information that stimulates further study and encourages the establishment of timely programs. The overarching goal is to increase awareness of the interdependence of all life – including all members of the family ecosystem, where acts of violence have resonating effects upon others.

As *Latham Letter* editor Judy Johns said in the groundbreaking video, *Breaking the Cycles of Violence,*

"When animals are abused, people are at risk. When people are abused, animals are at risk."

Latham rapidly became a leader in promoting awareness of The Link and of the many research findings, programmatic innovations, public policies, and community coalitions that began to develop locally, nationally and even internationally. On October 24, 1992, Latham organized a conference at Mills College in Oakland, Calif., entitled "A Cooperative Approach to the Prevention of Child and Animal Abuse: The Problem, Solutions, and Reality." The historic conference introduced 52 child and animal welfare professionals to the benefits of sharing information – for society, for their clients, and for themselves. Featured speakers, including noted actress Betty White, used the solution-oriented forum to encourage cross-training and cross-reporting between disciplines.

In February, 1993, Latham officials met in Denver, Colo., and determined that the prevention of child and animal abuse would be a high priority. A task force, the Child and Animal Abuse Prevention Project (CAAP), was created. Ad hoc committee members were Phil Arkow, Chair, with Frank Ascione, Mary Pat Boatfield, and Robert ten Bensel, all highly respected authorities. They were often in demand as speakers and authors, and they carried the Latham Link message forward to countless animal welfare and human services professionals around the world.

In 1994 Latham underwrote the production costs of *Working with Families in Shelters: A Practical Guide for Counselors and Child Care Staff,* by Lynn Loar and John H. Weakland. Through this support, 1,000 shelters for homeless families were able to receive, free of charge, guidance on working with adults and children and dealing with various forms of abuse.

Working with Families in Shelters:

A Practical Guide for Counselors and Child Care Staff

WRITTEN BY

Lynn Loar, *San Francisco Child Abuse Council*
John H. Weakland, *Mental Research Institute*

5. WATERSHED PUBLICATIONS

A needs assessment survey of 500 leaders in numerous fields resulted in Latham's 1995 publication, *Breaking the Cycles of Violence*. This 62-page training manual and accompanying 26-minute video redefined animal abuse as not an isolated incident with only an animal victim, but rather as an under-recognized component of family violence with serious implications for multiple victims and for society as well. The video and manual were designed for use by community groups, coalitions, educators, and professional training and development. The package was priced modestly low to be affordable for nonprofit agencies. Latham hoped that the insidious cycles of violence enveloping families could be broken by concerted, cooperative community-wide efforts that must include animal care and control professionals previously ignored in such coalitions.

The original *Breaking the Cycles of Violence* and its updated 2003 version were widely distributed internationally. Today many hundreds of copies continue to be sold, and *Cycles II* continues to be the Foundation's most widely-distributed video.

Following the great success of *Cycles,* Latham's next major project was a textbook – an anthology of essays on The Link. This source book would be similar to two prior animal-assisted therapy texts, *Dynamic Relationships in Practice: Animals in the Helping Professions,* published in 1984, and *The Loving Bond: Companion Animals in the Helping Professions,* published in 1987. Though now out of print, these texts are still widely regarded as seminal resource tools. As was the case with the two earlier books, Phil Arkow served as editor, and Frank Ascione was brought in as co-editor to provide additional academic credentials. The result was *Child Abuse, Domestic Violence, and Animal Abuse: Linking the Circles of*

Compassion for Prevention and Intervention. This 479-page compilation of 47 essays by 50 prominent authors was published in 1999 by the Purdue University Press, whose extensive library of human-animal bond titles is world-renowned. The book's goal was to disseminate as widely as possible Link information in a quality, well-respected publication. In this regard the book continues to achieve its goal admirably, and today still enjoys robust distribution worldwide and serves as a standard reference work.

In the Foreword, Hugh H. Tebault, II (1917 – 2007), Director Emeritus of Latham, noted that the proliferation of specialized institutions and charities to care for society's needy was a two-edged sword: individualized services allowed for greater resources and opportunities to help those in need, but paradoxically specialists had lost track of the common bonds that formerly united them in a continuum of care. Child protection workers need to be reminded that their work originated in the animal protection movement; domestic violence workers need to be made aware that their work affects children, he noted. All need to consider whether animals may be affected by other forms of family violence. As distinct service delivery systems have emerged, it is unfortunately too easy for practitioners to overlook the common denominators affecting their work. "The abatement of cruelty is dramatically enhanced by direct cooperation between responsible human and animal welfare agencies," he wrote.

Child Abuse, Domestic Violence, and Animal Abuse brought together, for the first time, social workers and lawyers, prosecutors and veterinarians, animal shelter personnel and child welfare caseworkers, domestic violence officials and domestic violence survivors. The book was born of diversity. It offered a forum for researchers with their studies, philosophers with their dreams, program leaders with their strategies, and survivors with their remarkable courage to speak out. Some wrote with statistical perspectives; others wrote with heartfelt passion. Some theorized; others vividly depicted horrifying first-person accounts. The textbook featured philosophical concerns and practical solutions. It aimed to be provocative and to raise more questions than it answered. It concluded with an extensive list of research, public policy and programmatic recommendations that are still being worked on today. Latham was confident that the book would appeal to educators and professionals in many fields, and our expectations were more than realized.

"Collaborative, multidisciplinary approaches clearly open new horizons in the areas of understanding and reducing aggression toward humans and other animals," Arkow and Ascione wrote. "Recognizing and achieving our common goals remain challenging and daunting – but not impossible – tasks."

6. THE *LATHAM LETTER* AND THE LINK

Latham's quarterly magazine, *The Latham Letter,* has been publishing thoughtful articles of interest to an ever-widening circle of readers concerned with human-animal interactions since 1980. The Foundation was quick to dedicate a significant amount of editorial space to The Link. *The Latham Letter* serves as a major disseminator of vital information about this critical topic. Since 1987, more than 120 Link articles have been published: some have reported original research, others have described programs in action, while still others have reported on important conferences and historic legislation. The result has been a dramatic increase in the number of individuals and organizations working together to promote kindness to all living things.

Early articles in the 1980s began to hint at what was to emerge as a full-fledged focus. "Animal Abuse Ties to Crime" and "Working toward Prevention of Child Abuse and Neglect" were two of five Link-themed articles in the Summer, 1987 issue.

The Summer, 1992 issue unleashed what was to become a steady stream of new information. Robert ten Bensel and Michael Robin of the University of Minnesota put the abuse of animals and children into a historical perspective. Lynn Loar and Kenneth White described their pioneering Humane Coalition

Against Violence in the San Francisco Bay Area. Phil Arkow and Cathy Rosenthal reported on the American Humane Association's first national summit on violence towards children and animals.

The Spring, 1994 issue was devoted to the direct relationship that non-human cruelty has to human violence. "The Latham Foundation is taking a leadership role in sensitizing its readers and various professional communities to the Links between violence against children, animals, and other vulnerable members of society," President Hugh H. Tebault II wrote. "It is doing this for a variety of reasons. Partly it is in response to the fact that the compartmentalized efforts of humane and human service agencies haven't worked. Partly it is a 'back to the basics' approach to view child and animal abuse in the entire continuum of community violence. And finally, it is because of Latham's expertise positions to make this connection and actually do something about the rising tide of violence."

By the Winter of 1995 *The Latham Letter* was presenting practical tips, publishing a list of "What You Can Do to Stop the Cycle of Abuse and Neglect," and presenting "Four Warning Signs That Should Concern Parents." Readers were able to learn about the proceedings of six regional Link conferences. The concept of providing foster care for pets belonging to domestic violence survivors was first described in a Winter, 1996 article about the Loudoun County, Virginia, cooperative program between the abused women's shelter, the humane society, and animal control. By the Spring of 1996 readers could learn about therapeutic interventions with children who had been abused, neglected, or at risk of violence. Over the years, similar articles would spotlight such noteworthy interventions as New Mexico's Project Second Chance, California's Forget-Me-Not Farm, South Carolina's Crossroads group home, the Los Angeles SPCA's TLC program, and Cincinnati's Strategic Humane Interventions Program for battered women and their children.

As the 1990s drew to a close, *Latham Letter* readers could learn about new cross-reporting and mandatory counseling laws, domestic violence interventions in the Baltimore Police Department, Link training programs and community coalitions in five states, assistance programs for the pet survivors of domestic violence, and animal-assisted therapy for victims of child sexual abuse.

The horrific tragedies at Littleton, Colo.'s, Columbine High School prompted a Fall, 1999 review of five such incidents in which unspeakable acts of animal cruelty and torture presaged armed youths' killing sprees in schools.

Increased public and professional awareness about the connections between animal abuse and family/community violence led to public policy initiatives. *Latham Letter* readers could quickly learn about the latest laws. such as mandated counseling for cruelty offenders, cross-reporting mandates, and increased felony penalties for animal cruelty offenses.

As the new millennium dawned, readers could see how global Latham's interests and outreach had become. Phil Arkow's lecture and media tour of South Africa helped local animal advocates initiate a national humane education initiative based upon the Link theme. The South African humane education curriculum remains a living testimonial to the power of what a few dedicated individuals can accomplish.

Meanwhile, Canadian groups began conducting widespread Link efforts. Veterinary reporting of animal cruelty, Link conferences, and violence prevention coalitions were organized across Canada. Research was undertaken, cross-reporting programs were launched, and training conferences were held in the United Kingdom, Brazil, and Hungary.

Latham produced its own training books and videos and *The Latham Letter* alerted readers to other

Link resources available: a training video for law enforcement officers; guides for housing the animal survivors of domestic violence; coalition start-up guides; Link-themed humane education curricula; materials for prosecutors and veterinarians; a video to help communities develop animal hoarding task forces; and informative public awareness posters from Baltimore, Washington, Detroit, and Omaha.

Latham continued taking readers into new, exciting territory. Dr. Randall Lockwood introduced readers to the connections between animal cruelty and elder abuse as early as 2002. Phil Arkow compiled the first summary of cross-reporting policies endorsed by national veterinary associations in the U.S., Canada, U.K., and New Zealand. How The Link affects rural communities was first brought to readers' attention in 2003. Ken Shapiro described in 2005 the empathy-based AniCare and AniCare Child treatment programs for perpetrators of animal cruelty. Readers learned in 2005 of "Cut Out Domestic Violence" programs in Florida and Virginia where beauty salons offer safe space and resources to battered women.

A list of *Latham Letter* authors who have written about The Link includes prominent pioneers and leaders. Contributors include Phil Arkow, Frank Ascione, Lesley Ashworth, Barbara W. Boat, Mary Pat Boatfield, Craig Daniell, Deborah Doherty, Tom Flanagan, Jennie Hornosty, Lisa Lembke, Lynn Loar, Randall Lockwood, Sue McIntosh, Chris Risley-Curtiss, Cathy Rosenthal, Ken Shapiro, Betsy Sikora Siino, Robert ten Bensel, Bob Walter, and Kenneth White.

In response to growing worldwide interest in accessing these critical articles, Latham has converted many of them to PDFs and posted them in an online archive at http://www.latham.org

7. NEW HORIZONS

With growing global interest in The Link, Latham continues to remain a prime source for information, materials, and intelligent perspective. In 2004 Latham published *Teaching Empathy: Animal-Assisted Therapy Programs for Children and Families Exposed to Violence,* by Lynn Loar, Ph.D., LCSW, and Libby Colman, Ph.D. This handbook for therapists, teachers, and humane educators uses The Link as a basis for bringing animal-assisted interventions and humane education to troubled children. The manual is further proof of the collaborative ability of The Link to tie multiple interests together in a holistic approach to ending violence.

In 2008 Latham again actively participated in a national summit on The Link. The "Strategizing The Link" National Town Meeting and Experts' Summit in Portland, Maine, resulted in the formation of the National Link Coalition.

Latham offered its services to provide the initial hosting of the Coalition's web site. Latham is active in helping the new Coalition promote interagency cooperation and facilitate the collection of information, resources, and progress being made. Latham helped sponsor the Coalition's subsequent 2010 and 2012 Summit meetings, both held in Denver, Colo., to assist in strategic planning and program development for this important initiative.

8. WHAT LATHAM BELIEVES

"In the hearts of little children

Lies a tenderness and love

For all of nature's creatures

That is given from above.

'Tis this feeling, wisely nurtured,

Trained to honesty and right,

Forms the first step on the pathway

Leading upward to the light."

-- from The Steps, by Dolores Wilkens Kent (circa 1930)

Latham's focus on promoting respect for all life through education, particularly the education of children, has taken many forms over the decades. The need to respect animals and each other transcends generations, even though the message, methods, and technology used to teach these values may change. In recent years Latham has recognized that humane education includes respect for the human-animal bond, appreciation for animal-assisted therapy, and the prevention of family violence. Expanding the focus continues a nearly century-old tradition of advancing humane education by adapting the message to an evolving society.

But one thing has remained constant: Latham uses its resources to highlight the importance of universal kinship for all life. Latham sees humane education –

with its emphasis on empathy, altruism, gentleness, honesty, kindness, and self-confidence – as a core value and a positive force that supports other societal values.

Like many humane organizations, Latham is frequently asked why it concentrates on animal welfare when there are so many pressing human welfare concerns in the world. Latham subscribes to the premise that animal issues are human welfare concerns as well. The primitive world is still very much alive within us; we are interconnected with the forces of nature around us, and what affects the world of nature affects the human species as well. In the midst of the evolution of human experience, animals can bring a sense of calm, representing a world more tuned to nature's cycles, instinct, sensation, awareness, subtleties of body language, and intuition. Animals stimulate us not only by touch, but by some deeply buried aspect of nature within us, a connection to part of something greater, more healthy, and more whole. Most of us have become separated from our natural, instinctual selves – the part of us that can proudly, not disparagingly, be called animal. Animals help us to reconnect with our inner core, reminding us of our connections with our more primitive ancestors and that we are part of the universe as a whole. It is in these connections we see what we share in common, rather than what separates us, and our innate drive for relationship is satisfied.

Latham has long believed that establishing humane communities is too large a process for any one organization or field to undertake alone. Consequently, Latham promotes the value of strategic alliances and non-partisanship that can build collaborative projects. Great good can occur when respected agencies in multiple fields complement each other by working together in areas of common agreement to achieve greater good for those who cannot speak for themselves.

Recognizing that positive reinforcement works much better than negative, and that consensus is stronger than polarization, Latham traditionally has reported "good news." Latham does not create community programs: rather, it promotes such programs as highly effective utilization of resources and as embodiments of their belief that respect is a two-way street.

Latham serves as a catalyst for responsible thought and action, a neutral, non-threatening convener that generates involvement. It is widely respected for its balanced perspective on humane issues and activities. The Link is an example of uniting otherwise disparate organizations into an area of common interest where they are able to share the stage together.

The many community programs and coalitions that have emerged in the past 20 years to explore the connections between animal abuse and human violence dramatically demonstrate this principle. While each group has its specialized interests and reasonable differences of opinion are inevitable, by communicating openly and working together they can agree to disagree on some areas and concentrate on areas of common ground. This intersection of interests brings the best contributions of each participant to create a larger, more cohesive and more accepted outcome.

The wide use of Latham's materials over the decades by so many different types of humane and human services agencies is particularly gratifying. Latham trusts that cooperation between child and animal welfare agencies, domestic violence and adult protective services, law enforcement and the courts, veterinarians, human medical professionals, and so many others will continue. As a result, neglect and violence will be reduced.

But building a humane society is not solely a process for institutions, organizations, or government agencies. The best place to stop problems is at home. Latham's long-standing premise is that if children learn respect for all creatures early in life, they will grow up with core values that produce respect for others, the community, the nation, and the world. Other cherished values – the importance of good citizenship, neighborliness, pride in our communities, and watching out for the welfare of others – all flow from this simple premise. As Edith Latham wrote in the late 1940s in the Foundation's publication, *The Gateway,* "The work promotes the mental and moral growth in the thousands of children we contact; it raises the standard of citizenship in youth, so greatly needed today."

It is up to each of us, in our own towns and cities, to take personal responsibility. Those who observe cruel behaviors must stop the cycle of violence at its earliest stages. All of us must take individual responsibility to reject any cruelty as a clearly unacceptable behavior. Latham believes that if everyone recognized their personal responsibilities and carried them out with an attitude of kindness toward one another, all of us – humans, animals, and communities – would be better for it.

As a force of reason in the midst of high emotions and dramatic passions regarding animals and children, Latham recognizes that changing community values takes much time and commitment. Progress in humane education is measured in small, incremental steps. Not expecting immediate change, Latham takes a longer, more practical view. Latham sees humane education as a frontier practice: despite a rich history and wealth of experience, Latham often has to go where seemingly few have gone before. In this regard, Latham has secured a reputation as perennially being ahead of its time.

This process of slow, steady growth was expressed by the late Nathania Gartman in a 2002 *Latham Letter* article:

- Recognize that culture is complex.
- Educate yourself.
- Treat others the way you want to be treated.
- Participate in the community.
- Teach the facts.
- Be patient.
- Above all, be kind.

Latham's focus has always been preventive rather than corrective. The Foundation endeavors to project human sensibilities forward to the degree that the need for such valuable social services agencies as animal shelters, child protection agencies, and domestic violence shelters is diminished.

———

We must individually raise the bar of acceptable behavior if we as a culture are to be happy, healthy, and humane.

———

Societal values and civility are, fundamentally, what hold us together. The Latham Foundation was started to promote humane education – kindness to animals and to each other. This is a noble cause, but it can succeed only if it is built upon a foundation of society's shared vision of right and wrong, of compassion and of personal responsibility. Teaching benevolence, respect and kindness to animals and to each other is the natural starting point for personal growth and responsibility. We must individually raise the bar of acceptable behavior if we as a culture are to be happy, healthy, and humane.

There is more than enough work remaining for all of us to do, and Latham is proud to be a small part of the solution. Latham welcomes your interest and your ideas for serving your needs and working together to protect animals and people.

APPENDIX 1: LATHAM AND THE LINK — A CHRONOLOGY

1991 – Latham participates in the first national summit on The Link, sponsored by the American Humane Association in November in Denver, Colo. This watershed event brings together 30 national leaders from child and animal welfare in a call to action addressing research, education, programmatic and treatment issues.

1992 – Latham participates in the second American Humane summit, held in September in Herndon, Vir. More than 100 participants discuss "Protecting Children and Animals: Agenda for a Non-Violent Future." Lawyers, pediatricians, nurses, theologians, teachers, psychologists and animal welfare professionals attend. Many come away from the two-day conference with a "Eureka!" moment because they had never thought of their responsibility or ability to prevent child and animal abuse by being aware of both. Vital connections are made, and new understandings reached, in strengthening the new chain of determination to prevent child and animal abuse.

1992 – Latham sponsors a groundbreaking conference on October 24 at Mills College in Oakland, Calif., to encourage cross-training and cross-reporting between animal and child protection professionals. "A Cooperative Approach to the Prevention of Child and Animal Abuse" opens the eyes of many advocates and professionals to the interrelationship of various forms of family violence.

1993 – In February, Latham creates a task force, the Child and Animal Abuse Prevention Project (CAAP), (later renamed the Family Violence

Prevention Project) to promote and implement cooperative programs involving child and animal welfare and domestic violence prevention agencies. CAAP advisory committee members are Phil Arkow, Chair, with Frank Ascione, Mary Pat Boatfield, and Robert ten Bensel, all highly respected authorities. They carry the Latham Link message forward to countless animal welfare and human services professionals around the world at meetings and conferences. They are frequently in demand as speakers and authors.

1994 – Latham publishes *Working with Families in Shelters: A Practical Guide for Counselors and Child Care Staff,* by Lynn Loar and John H. Weakland. The book introduces staffs at shelters for the homeless, addicted and domestic violence survivors to their responsibilities to identify and report various forms of abuse and neglect.

1995 – Latham publishes *Breaking the Cycles of Violence*, a unique 62-page training manual by Phil Arkow and an accompanying 26-minute video, which redefine animal abuse not as an isolated incident with only an animal victim, but rather as an under-recognized component of family violence. The underlying message is that various forms of family violence stem from the same origins and motivations, and therefore all family members are at risk

"This is me and my cat. My dad treats my cat unfairly, like he treats my mom." Jennifer, Age 8

whenever anyone is abused. *Cycles* introduces professionals in child protection, animal welfare and domestic violence prevention to strategies to identify all forms of family violence and to cooperate in effective community-based programs.

1996 – The *Cycles* video wins the coveted first-place Maxwell Award from the Dog Writers' Association of America for Best Video and Excellence in Videotape Production. Child and Animal Abuse Prevention Project advisors present Link training in Israel, Ireland, Japan, Washington D.C., Arizona, California, Michigan, New Jersey, Oregon, Texas, Wisconsin, West Virginia, Ohio, Utah, and Rhode Island. Latham multiplies its outreach, inaugurating a web site, www.latham.org.

1997 – *Breaking the Cycles of Violence* serves as the core of many child and animal welfare conferences and police departments' training. Its basic message resonates widely among audiences. *Cycles* is featured on the Oprah Winfrey TV show.

1998 – A strategic planning session includes The Link as a primary focus for Latham. Latham speakers present Link training across the U.S. and to the International Association of Human-Animal Interaction organizations, meeting in Prague, Czech Republic.

1999 – A three-year project culminates with the publication of Latham's commissioned anthology, *Child Abuse, Domestic Violence, and Animal Abuse: Linking the Circles of Compassion for Prevention and Intervention,* by Purdue University Press. This groundbreaking 479-page textbook, edited by Phil Arkow and Frank Ascione, Ph.D., includes 47 original essays by 50 authorities in numerous fields and by survivors of family violence.

1999 – Latham publishes *Teaching Compassion: A Guide for Humane Educators, Teachers, and Parents,* by Pamela Raphael, Libby Colman, Ph.D., and Lynn Loar, Ph.D. This manual and its accompanying lesson plans train educators to recognize signs of animal cruelty and neglect, and provide them with skills to respond to children's disclosures of abuse.

2000 – CAAP members continue to reach new audiences as varied at the Swedish Kennel Club, England's University of Cambridge veterinary college, the International Society for Anthrozoology in The Netherlands, a violence prevention initiative in South Africa, the Canadian Federation of Humane Societies, the American Veterinary Medical Association's annual conference, the Florida State Child Abuse Prevention Conference, and the National Conference on Domestic Violence.

2000 – The Edith Latham Award for Excellence in Video Productions Promoting Respect for All Life is awarded to the Chicago Anti-Cruelty Society and filmmaker Erik Friedl for their dramatic program,

Patterns of Abuse: Exploding the Cycle. This video quickly becomes a key audio-visual presentation describing The Link.

2001 – Latham Link speakers provide training at numerous national and international conferences. New audiences reached include military family services agencies at a U.S. Air Force base in Florida; an Attorney General's task force in Delaware; the Wyoming Coalition Against Domestic Violence and Sexual Assault Conference; the Michigan Judicial Institute; a province-wide violence prevention conference in Ontario; the College of Veterinary Medicine at Oklahoma State University; a child abuse summit in Oregon; the International Family Violence Research Conference in New Hampshire; and a community college in New York. As a result of a Latham-sponsored presentation by Lynn Loar at the International Conference on Child Abuse and Neglect, the U.S. Office of Criminal Justice Planning awards a grant of $250,000 per year for three years for the Strategic Humane Intervention Program (SHIP).

2002 – In the wake of the September 11, 2001 tragedies, the guiding principles set forth by Edith and Milton Latham appear even more relevant. The Edith Latham Award for Excellence in Video Productions Promoting Respect for All Life is given to Albuquerque's Project Second Chance, a unique animal-assisted therapeutic intervention for adolescents at risk of violence.

2003 – In response to popular demand and in the interest of providing the most useful and comprehensive resources available, the pioneering *Breaking the*

Cycles of Violence manual and video are updated. The guide to multi-disciplinary interventions gives child welfare, animal care and control, and domestic violence prevention professionals additional tangible tools to identify, report and manage cases of abuse and neglect. A total of 564 copies are distributed in the first year.

2004 – Latham publishes *Teaching Empathy: Animal-Assisted Therapy Programs for Children and Families Exposed to Violence,* by Lynn Loar, Ph.D., LCSW, and Libby Colman, Ph.D. This handbook for therapists, teachers, and humane educators uses The Link as a basis for bringing animal-assisted interventions and humane education to troubled children, and serves as further testimony to the collaborative ability of The Link to tie multiple interests together in a holistic approach to ending violence.

2005 – Latham breaks new ground and discovers new Link audiences – a statewide conference of probation and parole officers in Delaware, and a Link conference in Budapest, Hungary. The SHIP program is implemented as a seven-week intervention at a transitional living facility for battered women and their children in Cincinnati.

2006 – Maine enacts the nation's first law allowing judges to include pets in domestic violence protection-from-abuse orders; Vermont and New York quickly follow. *The Latham Letter* reports on these developments and other key Link laws in West Virginia, Kansas, and Tennessee.

2008 – Latham actively participates in the third national summit on The Link, held in Portland, Maine. The "Strategizing The Link" National Town Meeting and Experts' Summit results in the formation of the National Link Coalition. Latham hosts the first web site and list serve to help the new organization launch its national collaborative efforts and to facilitate the collection of information, resources and progress.

2009 – Due to great, ongoing interest, Latham compiles an archive of *Latham Letter* articles about the Link and places them on its website to assist researchers seeking data.

2010 – Latham co-sponsors the National Link Coalition's Roundtable and organizational Summit meeting at the University of Denver's Graduate School of Social Work.

2011 – *The Latham Letter* spotlights the innovative Link-based violence prevention program and women's shelter kennels for the animal victims of domestic violence developed by Child Abuse Prevention in Klamath County, Oregon.

2011 – A unique curriculum bringing Link training to law enforcement officers is posted online at Latham's website.

2012 – Latham compiles a history of its extensive involvement with the connections between animal abuse and other forms of family violence.

2012 – Latham sponsors the National Link Coalition's strategic planning Summit meeting at a National Coalition Against Domestic Violence's biennial conference in Denver, Colo.

APPENDIX 2: LIST OF *LATHAM LETTER* LINK ARTICLES THROUGH 2012

PLEASE VISIT THE RESEARCH & RESOURCES PAGE AT
WWW.LATHAM.ORG
FOR RECENT ENTRIES.

Conferences	Research	Programs	Coalitions	Legislation	General Link Info
Child and Animal Abuse Prevention Seminar Attracts Concerned Professionals (Mills College) – Winter 93	*American Humane Assn. releases Report on its Nov. 1991 Summit on Violence Towards Children and Animals* – Summer 92	*Child Abuse Reporting Hotline Falls Short* — Winter 93	*Connections Drawn Between Child and Animal Victims of Violence* (S.F. Humane Coalition Against Violence) – Summer 92	*Statewide Commission Created for Cross-Reporting Legislation* (Rhode Island) – Summer 97	*Cruelty: Where do We Draw the Line?* — Summer 87
List of Forthcoming Link Training Conferences – Spring 94	*Link Between Animal cruelty and Child Abuse Described at AHA Summit* – Summer 92	*A Humane Garden of Children, Plants and Animals Grows in Sonoma County, Calif.* – Spring 94	*The Shape of Cruelty* (S.F. Humane Coalition Against Violence) – Summer 92	*Rhode Island Commission Sets Example for Other States: How a Single Comment Benefits Thousands of Children and Animals* – Spring 98	*Animal Abuse Ties to Crime* – Summer 87
Wisconsin Coalition Organizes Anti-Abuse Conference (La Crosse, WI) – Summer 94	*A Test for Determining Why Children are Cruel to Animals* — Summer 93	*Washington, D.C. Humane Society Link Poster* – Winter 95	*Animal Advocates Looking Out for Children* (Toledo) Fall 93	*Legislative Update: California and Oregon Enact Link Laws* – Winter 99	*An Overview of Child Protective Services* – Summer 87

Conferences	Research	Programs	Coalitions	Legislation	General Link Info
Israel Conference Puts The Link Between Animal and Child Abuse on the Public Agenda (Concern for Helping Animals in Israel) – Summer 94	*Bedwetting, Fire Setting, and Animal Cruelty* – Spring 94	*Working to Break the Cycles of Violence* (Los Angeles SPCA TLC) Spring 95	*Tacoma, Washington's Humane Coalition Perseveres in the Fight Against Family and Community Violence* – Winter 95	*Link Legislation Compiled* (by Animal Legal Defense Fund) Fall 99	*Dangerous Dogs: A Symptom of Dangerous People* – Fall 89
Animal Cruelty and The Link to Other Violent Crimes: Utah Conference on Companion Animals in Crisis Surprises Participants – Winter 95	*Animal Abuse and Domestic Violence: Intake Statistics Tell a Sad Story* – Spring 94	*Michigan Humane Society Link Poster* Summer 95	*San Diego Child Protection Services Workers Now Required to Report Animal Abuse* – Summer 95	*Providing Treatment for People Who Hurt Animals: California's New Law* – Winter 00	*Compassion for All Creatures: Putting the Abuse of Ani-mals and Children in Historical Perspective* — Summer 92
USC Conference Addresses Violence Against Children – Spring 95	*Cruelty to Animals as One of the Predictors of Serial Killers* — Summer 94	*Abuse an Animal – Go to Jail!* (Animal Legal Defense Fund Resources for Prosecutors* – Summer 95	*The "Web of Hope" Grows Stronger* (Rhode Island Windwalker Humane Coalition) – Fall 96	*States with Felony Animal Cruelty Provisions* – Spring 02	*Upsetting Comparisons* (Between child and animal cruelty investigations) – Summer 92
The Tangled Web: Animal Cruelty and Family Violence – Wisconsin Coalition Moves Forward (La Crosse) — Spring 95	*Survey Yields Surprising Results: Child & Animal Abuse Prevention Needs Assessment* – Summer 94	*Latham Lauds Alpha Affiliates, Morristown, NJ* – Fall 95	*New England Animal Control/Humane Task Force* (Boston Child Witness to Violence project) Spring/Summer 99	*Groundbreaking Legislation in Great Britain: British Vets Take Major Step Forward in Reporting Suspected Family Violence* Spring 03	*I Befriended a Child Molester* – Spring 93
Child and Animal Abuse Prevention Conference Summaries: Troy, MI; La Crosse, WI; Providence, RI; Glen Dale, WV; Somerset, NJ – Summer 95	*Domestic Violence and Cruelty to Animals* (Utah Women's Shelters Survey) – Winter 96	*Latham Lauds A Shelter for Battered Women's Pets, Loudoun County, VA* – Winter 96	*Link Coalitions Engaging Community Groups in Five States* (OR, IL, IN, FL, OH) – Fall 99	*Good News:* (California Veterinarians mandated to report animal abuse) – Winter 05	*Latham confronts Child and Animal Abuse* – Spring 94

Conferences	Research	Programs	Coalitions	Legislation	General Link Info
	Born to Abuse? Why Boys Are More Likely Than Girls to Hurt Animals and Others – Winter 99	I Liked the Policeman Who Arrested that Dog! (San Francisco therapeutic interventions with violent, abused and neglected children) – Spring 96	From the Maryland Family Violence Council – Concerning The Link – Spring 2001	The Link: Good News from Oregon – Summer 2011	A Shared Cry: Animal and Child Abuse Connections – Fall 94
Latham's C.A.A.P. Represented at the 11th National Conference on Child Abuse and Neglect – Winter 97	A Wealth of Information on The Link Between Violence to People and Animals: American Humane Association Children's Division – Fall 99	A Boy and His "Shiloh" Dog (The Shiloh Project, Fairfax, VA) – Summer 96	Putting the Link All Together: Ontario SPCA's Violence Prevention Initiative – Spring 01		What You Can Do to Stop the Cycle of Abuse and Neglect – Winter 95
Latham Represented at the 12th National Conference on Child Abuse and Neglect – Winter 99	Ontario SPCA's Women's Shelter Survey Shows Staggering Results – Spring 01	The Domestic Violence Assistance Program Protects Women, Children and Their Pets in Lane County, OR – Summer 97	Making a Difference for People and Animals in Hamilton, Ontario – Winter 03		Animal Cruelty IS Domestic Violence - Winter 96
Latham Foundation Sponsors Symposium at British Columbia Conference, "Creating a Legacy of Hope" – Winter 2009	Calgary Research: Exploring The Links Between Animal Abuse and Domestic Violence – Fall 01	University of Pennsylvania Veterinary Hospital Initiates Abuse Reporting Policy – Fall 97	New Training Materials Help Professionals Recognize Non-Accidental Animal Injury (UK coalition) – Spring 03		And Kindness for ALL (Massachusetts SPCA Viewpoint on The Link) – Summer 96
Latham's Link Message Goes to South Africa – Spring 2000	Examining Ontario's Link Between Child & Animal Welfare Sum04	Shelters Making a Difference (Eugene, OR; San Francisco, CA) – Spring 98	Partnerships Formed in Colorado to Stop the Cycle of Abuse – Sum 04		Dimensions of the Human-Animal Bond – Summer 96

Conferences	Research	Programs	Coalitions	Legislation	General Link Info
Humane Education, Rural Domestic Violence Focus of Link Symposiums in Canada – Summer 03	Pet-Abuse.com is Breaking the Cycle of Violence through Action, Education, and Information – Spring 05	Confronting Abuse (by a Veterinarian) – Summer 98	National Town Meeting and Summit to Strategize National, Local Link Efforts – Spring 08		Part of What Veterinarians Do is Treat Animal Victims of Violence: Should they Also Report Abusers? Fall 96
Tulane University Symposium Introduces The Link to Lawyers – Spring 04	Important Online Resource: Bibliography of The Link – Winter 08	Baltimore Police Department Links Animal Abuse and Domestic Violence Winter 99	Link Coalition Launched in Connecticut – Summer 09		An Update on The Link – Fall 96
Nova Scotia Conference Explores The Link – Summer 04	Exploring The Links: Firearms, Family Violence & Animal Abuse in Rural Communities – Summer 08	Nebraska Humane Society Link Poster Spring/Sum 99	Putting the Link to Work at the Local Level: Mine's Linkage Project Moves beyond Theory – Spring 2010		The Relationship Between Animal Abuse and Other Forms of Family Violence – Winter 97
Latham Brings LINK Training to Brazilian Police Officers – Winter 05	Confronting Animal Abuse: Law, Criminology and Human-Animal Relationships – Summer 2010	Resources: First Strike Campaign – Fall 99	Supporting the Link in New Mexico: Making Strides to Address Human and Animal Abuse – Fall 2011		The Human-Animal Abuse Connection – Spring 98
Link Activities Extend to Delaware's Probation and Parole Officers – Spring 05		Crossroads – An Intensive Treatment Program for Adolescent Girls (Sexual Abuse Victims) – Fall 2000	Animal Abuse is Everybody's Business – Winter 2011		What to Do If You're a Victim Spring 98

Conferences	Research	Programs	Coalitions	Legislation	General Link Info
Link Activities Come to the Windy City – Summer 05		Clicker Training with At-Risk Families Succeeds at the Humane Society of Santa Clara Valley – Fall 2000	Hands & Words Are Not for Hurting – Spring 2011		1997 – 1999 School Shootings Roundup – Fall 99
Latham Presents Link Message at Historic Hungarian Conference – Fall 05		The Ontario SPCA's Violence Prevention Initiative – Win 01			Review of The Violence Connection – Summer 2000
		South African Humane Education program Called "Overwhelmingly Positive" – Summer 01			Making the Connection Between Animal cruelty and Abuse and Neglect of Vulnerable Adults – Winter 02
		South Africa Leads the Way with National Humane Education Curriculum – Summer 02			Children and Animals: Exploring the Roots of Kindness and Cruelty – Fall 04
		New Link Resource Book for Albertans – Summer 02			Animal Cruelty: Pathway to Violence Against People – Spring 05
		Project Second Chance: Kids Helping Animals, Animals Helping Kids – Fall 02			Starting a Safe Havens for Animals Program and Creating Safer Communities for Older Adults and Companion Animals – Summer 05

Conferences	Research	Programs	Coalitions	Legislation	General Link Info
		Abuse: Why Cops Can, and Need, to Stop It (In the Line of Duty video for police) – Winter 03			*Children & Animals: Exploring the Roots of Kindness & Cruelty –* Spring 06
		Gabriel's Angels: Breaking the Cycles of Violence in Arizona – Summer 03			*Silent Victims: Recognizing and Stopping Abuse of the Family Pet –* Summer 06
		Identifying and Treating Animal Abuse: The AniCare Approach Winter 05			*10 things Teens Can Do to Help Stop Animal Cruelty –* Summer 08
		The Strategic Humane Interventions Positive Interactions to Battered Mothers and their Children in Cincinnati – Summer 05			*The International Handbook of Animal Abuse and Cruelty: Theory, Research, and Application –* Summer 08
		Canadian Veterinarians Adopt Strategic Policy on Reporting Animal Abuse – Summer 05			*The Link: The Devil is Back –* Winter 09
		Cut, Curl, and Counsel: Victims of Domestic Abuse Find Safe Haven at their Favorite Salon – Fall 05			*A Common Bond: Maltreated Children and Animals in the Home: Guide-lines for Practice and Policy –* Summer 09

Conferences	Research	Programs	Coalitions	Legislation	General Link Info
		Unique Online Course Teaches Illinois Law Enforcement Pro-fessionals about Animal Abuse – Fall 06			*The Cruelty Connection: The Relationships Between Animal Cruelty, Child Abuse, and Domestic Violence –* Spring 2001
		A Pet's Place Creates a Safe Haven Program for Pets of Women Who Are Battered – Fall 06			Link Training for Law Enforcement Officers Available Online Fall 2011
		Important Link cross-training resource: The Backup.com – Summer 08			*A Tragic Example of Agencies Not Communicating with Each Other* Spring 2012
		Children and Animals Together (CAT): Assessment and Diversion Program in Arizona – Summer 09			
		American Humane's Therapy Animals Supporting Kids (TASK) Program: How Animals Can Help Traumatized Children – Fall 10			

ABOUT THE AUTHOR

Internationally acclaimed lecturer, author, and educator Phil Arkow is a consultant and contributing editor to the Latham Foundation and chairs the Foundation's Animal Abuse and Family Violence Prevention Project. He is coordinator of the National Link Coalition and a consultant for the American Society for the Prevention of Cruelty to Animals and the Animals & Society Institute. He previously directed Link programs at the American Humane Association, the nation's oldest federation of child and animal protection organizations.

He was one of the founders of the National Link Coalition, the National Animal Control Association, the Animal Welfare Federation of New Jersey, and the Colorado Federation of Animal Welfare Agencies. He trains internationally on a variety of topics for animal shelters, child protection agencies, domestic violence programs, adult protective services, law enforcement, judges, and veterinarians. He is an adjunct faculty member at Harcum College in Pennsylvania and Camden County College in New Jersey where he teaches Certificate courses in Animal-Assisted Therapy.

A former newspaper reporter and foundation communications officer, Arkow is a prolific writer. He has authored and edited innumerable articles, chapters and 14 key reference books on the human-animal bond, violence prevention, humane education, animal-assisted therapy, and animal shelter management. He has also served with the American Veterinary Medical Association, the Delta Society, and the American Association of Human-Animal Bond Veterinarians.

Notes

www.ingramcontent.com/pod-product-compliance
Lightning Source LLC
Chambersburg PA
CBHW041514280526
45792CB00004B/1255